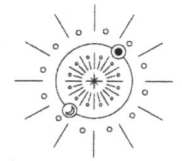

"Autumn is the time of reflection and gratitude. It is a season of quiet transformation, where the leaves fall, the light softens, and nature gently lets go.

Just as the trees surrender their leaves. So can we gather wisdom from the past, and prepare, with grace, for the stillness to come."

Teanna x

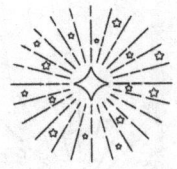

Dedicated to
my four amazing children -
the best gift I have ever received.
Cugs

www.TeannaTaylor.com

© Teanna Taylor 2025 All Rights Reserved

ISBN 978-1-917816-02-1

First Edition 2025

Published by TMJ Publishing

No part of this book may be copied or reproduced in any format, by any means, electronic or otherwise, without prior consent from the copyright owner and publisher.

This workbook is created and published for informational purposes only. It is not intended to be a substitute for professional medical advice and should not be relied on as health or personal advice. Always seek the guidance of your doctor or other qualified health professional with any questions you may have regarding your health or a medical condition.

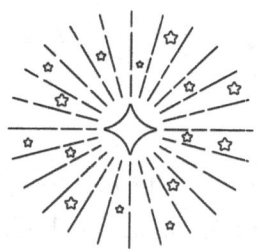

AUTUMN

**Cosmic Energy of:
Gratitude and Reflection**

This workbook aims to guide you in acknowledging your abundance with gratitude.

It accompanies the book 'Unlock Your Cosmic Flow'

Dates

22nd September 2025 - *Autumn Equinox*   30
- Overview of Now
- Find Your Soul Purpose
- Where Are You Now - Life Wheel
- Gratitude Jar
- Celebrate
- Meditation Online - 'Balance of Light and Dark'

From 29th September - First Quarter Moon   45
- Letter to future self

<u>7th October Hunters Full Moon</u>   47
- Reflection Inventory
- Preservation Letter
- Preserve Burial Ritual
- Meditation Online - 'Gratitude and Inner Strength'

From 13th October - Last Quarter Moon   54
- Cultivating Gratitude - Plan For Giving

From 20th October - New Moon   56
- Letters of Gratitude

From 27th October - First Quarter Moon   58
- Gratitude jar

<u>5th November Beaver Full Moon</u>   61
- Forming Foundations
- Inner Strengths Quiz
- Superpower Reflection
- Embedding Your Superpower in Daily Life
- Meditation Online - 'Roots of Stability'

Dates

From 12th November - Last Quarter Moon   72
- De-clutter

19th November - New moon   73
- Gather and Strengthen Resources

From 26th November - First Quarter Moon   75
- Focus on Self-Fulfilment
- ME Day

4th December - Cold Full Moon   78
- How do you handle stress - What is your Archetype?
- Stress Hexagon
- Full Moon Burn Ritual
- Meditation online - 'Letting Go of Stress'

From 11 December - Last Quarter Moon   79
- Reflecting on Personal Growth and Self Care

From 18th December - New Moon
- Reclaiming Your Power - Gift to Yourself   90

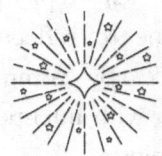

Introduction

Autumn gently reminds us of gratitude, abundance, the beauty in change and the wisdom in letting go. It teaches us to trust the process of transformation and is, by far, my favourite time of year. This is the season of harvest, both literal and symbolic - a culmination of the energy cycle and a preparation for the stillness and deep release of Winter. Autumn spans September through December and moves through three distinct energy flows, each aligning with the solar cycle and the Full Moons. It begins in September with the honouring of achievements, celebrating successes and growth.

While this stage should feel joyful, the heightened activity can sometimes lead to overwhelm if we are not grounded. Embracing the season's transformative energy with intention, presence, self-awareness, and self-care allows us to remain centred and balanced.

As October arrives and the leaves begin to fall, the days grow shorter and the energy subtly shifts. There is a quiet clarity in the air, a gentle invitation to slow down, to reflect, and to listen. In this stage, we are called to pause and examine the journey of the past cycle, acknowledging lessons learned, inner strengths and becoming aware of what no longer serves us. Reflection during this time reveals what has been working, what needs adjusting, and what must be released to create space for what is next. Letting go is rarely easy - it may involve processing emotions, shedding outdated beliefs or habits, and releasing attachments that have held us back. Yet these endings are not failures; they are sacred spaces where renewal quietly begins. Like trees releasing their leaves, we too must let go with intention, conserving our energy for what truly matters, preparing ourselves for the introspection of Winter and the quiet promise of new beginnings.

By November, the energy shifts once more toward slower, more deliberate movement. Self-care rises to the foreground, inviting us to honour the quieter pace the season asks of us. Grounding exercises, mindfulness, creative expression, and intentional rest help replenish energy, sharpen focus, and enhance creativity. This is a time to reflect on accomplishments, integrate lessons, and strengthen resilience. By committing to gratitude and honest reflection, we navigate the season with intention, honouring the work we have done and the person we are becoming.

December completes Autumn with gentle preparation for Winter. The energy winds down further, inviting deep reflection and closure. In this stage, we consciously gather the fruits of our labours and acknowledge growth. Full Moon meditations during this time offer additional alignment, helping us remain connected to cosmic rhythms while honouring our personal journey.

In Autumn, nature teaches us to celebrate growth and honour the journey we have undertaken. Each exercise in this season is designed to guide thoughtful reflection and foster gratitude:

- Harvest Your Accomplishments: Take stock of the seeds you planted and nurtured. Reflect on your achievements and recognise the progress you have made.
- Practice Gratitude: Deepen your appreciation for your journey, using gratitude to anchor your heart and mind in the abundance you have created.
- Reflect and Adjust: Consider what has worked well and where you might evolve your approach. Release what no longer serves you, making space for new growth.
- Cosmic Alignment: Engage with Full Moon meditations to support monthly reflection and alignment with natural and personal rhythms.
- Flexible Reflection: Autumn's pace is gentle and accommodating - if you need extra time to reflect or catch up, trust that the season will welcome you back.

Allow the reflective energy of Autumn to inspire you to celebrate your journey, honour your achievements, and prepare for new beginnings. Each step you take is a valuable part of your evolving manifestation, paving the way for even greater growth.

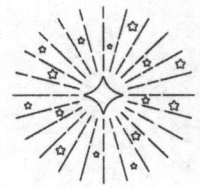

How To Use This Workbook

This workbook is designed to accompany the book
Unlock Your Cosmic Flow
This covers manifesting in line with the Cosmic Energy of the seasons in much more detail.

This workbook contains practical exercises, support and guidance to help you manifest your dreams while aligning with the Cosmic Energy of Autumn.

There are weekly tasks, three per each moon cycle, structured to be manageable and not overwhelming, then each full moon has a bespoke ritual, with more in-depth exercises, to boost personal energy aligned with that of the Cosmos. These pages are coloured grey for ease of finding.

Further guidance and support is available online on social media with top tips, and, of course, my meditations.

Follow the workbook week by week - the moon phases and full moon dates are at the top of the page. If you miss a week, just let it flow and catch up if you can. But try to stay on track with the full moons, for those are your natural energy boosts.

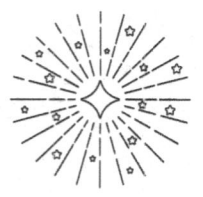

Key

General Information and Instructions

The Science Behind the Exercise

Exercise Start

Things You Will Need

Meditation On Line
www.TeannaTaylor.com

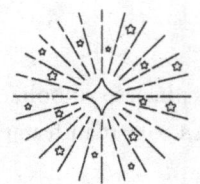

Introduction of moon cycles

The Moon goes through eight distinct phases as it orbits Earth. These phases are the different ways the Sun illuminates the Moon's surface from our point of view. It is important to note that the Moon itself does not produce light, so what we call 'moonlight' is simply sunlight reflecting off the Moon's surface.

The Sun always lights up half of the Moon, but from Earth we see different portions of that half depending on the Moon's position in its orbit. This orbit around Earth takes about 27.3 days, but because of the way Earth and Moon both move in relation to the Sun, it takes 29.5 days to go from one New Moon to the next.

The 8 Moon's Phases

- New Moon (●): The Moon is positioned between Earth and the Sun, so its sunlit side faces away from us. It appears completely dark.
- Waxing Crescent (●): A thin sliver of light becomes visible as the Moon moves away from the New phase.
- First Quarter (●): Half of the Moon's face is illuminated, creating the shape of a half-circle.
- Waxing Gibbous (●): More than half is lit, but it is not fully illuminated yet.
- Full Moon (○): The entire side facing Earth is illuminated, glowing as a bright circle.
- Waning Gibbous (●): The lit portion begins to shrink, though more than half is still visible.
- Last (Third) Quarter (●): Half of the Moon is visible again, but the opposite side compared to the First Quarter.
- Waning Crescent (●): Only a thin crescent remains before the cycle restarts at New Moon.

Symbolic Meaning

Across many cultures, the Moon's phases symbolize growth, release, and renewal. They are often linked to cycles of manifestation, guidance, and personal reflection.

For the purpose of this workbook, I'll simplify the cycle into four key phases. This will give you three exercises to complete between each Full Moon - roughly one per week. This will allow for the natural flow of energy and not be too burdensome to fit into your daily life.

Full Moon ( )   Last Quarter ( )

New Moon ( )   First Quarter ( )

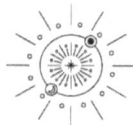

*"The moon does not fight.
It attacks no one. It does not worry.
It does not try to crush others.
It keeps to its course, but by its very nature, it gently influences.
What other body could pull an entire ocean from shore to shore?
The moon is faithful to its nature, and its power is never diminished."*

Ming-Dao Deng

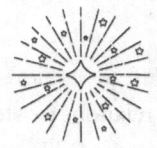

Working With Full Moon Energy

The energy of the full moon is at its peak on the night it becomes full, but its influence can be felt for a few days either side. Generally, you have a window of around five to seven days - approximately three days before and after the full moon - during which you can tune in easier, reflect, release, and set intentions. This is an ideal time to connect with your emotions, bring cycles to completion, and engage in rituals that support your personal growth and transformation.

There are several reasons why the energy feels heightened around the full moon, drawing from both scientific observations and spiritual traditions.

Firstly, the moon's gravitational pull influences the tides, and since the human body is largely composed of water, this pull subtly affects us too - impacting our emotional state, sleep patterns, and overall energy levels.

Secondly, the full moon is the brightest phase of the lunar cycle, symbolically casting light on what is usually hidden. This increased illumination is thought to bring clarity, amplify awareness, and intensify emotions.

Thirdly, the full moon marks the peak of the lunar cycle - a point of culmination. It represents the realisation of intentions set during the new moon, making it a powerful time for release, manifestation, and completion. The energetic surge at this phase can feel both intense and invigorating.

Throughout history and across cultures, the full moon has been regarded as a spiritually significant time. Many traditions recognise it as a potent moment for rituals, heightened intuition, and personal transformation. This collective belief may amplify the sense of energetic presence many people experience during this time.

Scientific studies have also begun to explore how the full moon influences human physiology, especially in relation to sleep and hormonal changes. For instance, research published in Current Biology found that during the full moon phase, participants experienced a 30% reduction in deep sleep, took longer to fall asleep, and slept for a shorter duration overall. Evening levels of melatonin (the hormone that regulates sleep) were also lower. These results, observed in controlled lab conditions, suggest a possible innate sensitivity to lunar cycles in humans.

Further studies found that Cortisol (the hormone associated with stress) tends to be higher, and some changes in blood components, such as increased haemoglobin levels in the evening, have also been observed.

Research has even highlighted cardiovascular effects. In one study of male university students, both resting and peak systolic blood pressure were found to be around 5 mmHg lower during the full and new moon phases compared to other times in the lunar cycle. Additionally, heart rate recovery after exercise was faster, suggesting a possible increase in physical efficiency during these phases.

While physiological effects are being increasingly documented, behavioural and psychological studies have yielded mixed results. Some research shows minimal or no significant changes in human behaviour linked to lunar phases, indicating that the effects we do notice may be more biological than behavioural.

More research is needed to fully understand how and why the full moon affects us, current evidence points to its influence on sleep quality, hormone levels, and even cardiovascular function. These findings complement long-held spiritual beliefs, offering a meaningful bridge between science and holistic practice.

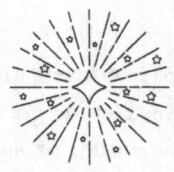

The Harvest Moon: A Gateway into Autumn

The Harvest Moon is not a full moon in its own right - the Corn Moon of September is often called the Harvest Moon, but it should be noted that the Harvest Moon rises each year as the full moon closest to the Autumn Equinox. This can either be the Corn Moon of September or the Hunters Moon of October. And can be different moons around the world, for example, in 2025, it falls in the UK on the September Corn Moon just before Autumn Equinox - the official beginning of Autumn on the 22nd September; however, due to the time difference, it falls in the USA on the October Hunters Moon.

Though it technically belongs to the final days of summer, its glow carries the unmistakable energy of autumn's arrival. It is a threshold moon, standing at the doorway between the abundance of summer and the descent into autumn's reflective embrace. It actually does not matter which moon the Harvest Moon falls on, as both the Corn and the Hunters moons carry the same energy - that of gratitude, preparation and abundance.

The Corn Moon symbolises a time to gather in the corn, nuts and berries and the Hunter moon symbolises a time to hunt way into the night and store meat, as the full moons illuminate the earth long into the night, giving extra time to gather crops and hunt before the darker half of the year begins.

Symbolically, they invite us to do the same within ourselves - under their light, we are called to celebrate our achievements, honour the fullness of our journey, and give thanks for the abundance we hold - whether in relationships, personal growth, creativity, or spiritual practice. At the same time, they whisper of what lies ahead: the gentle release, slowing down, and inner work that autumn brings.

Think of these moons as a sacred handover; a final burst of light and abundance before nature begins to shift toward letting go. By attuning to its energy, we step gracefully from the outward momentum of summer into the inward reflection of autumn, grounded, grateful, and ready to embrace the next stage of the cycle.

It is relatively rare for the Autumn Equinox and the Harvest Moon to occur so close together because the cycles that govern them operate on different timelines. The equinox is determined by the Earth's orbit around the Sun, marking the exact moment when day and night are nearly equal, which happens once a year. The Harvest Moon, on the other hand, follows the lunar cycle, occurring roughly every 29.5 days. Because the lunar month does not align perfectly with the solar year, full moons shift gradually throughout the calendar, so only occasionally does a full moon fall immediately before or after the equinox. This near alignment creates a unique convergence of solar and lunar energies, making the pairing of the Autumn Equinox and Harvest Moon a rare and special occurrence in any given year. The last time this happened was in 2010, when the Harvest Moon actually fell on the night of the Autumnal Equinox itself - September 22nd. This was the first time in nearly 20 years that such a near-perfect coincidence occurred, and it will not happen again until 2029.

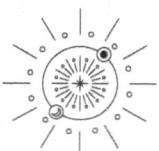

"The Harvest Moon rises, opening the golden gate from summer's warmth into autumn's embrace."

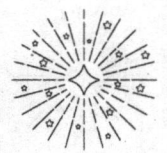

Equinox Vs Solstice
The Sun's Natural Cycle

Equinox happens twice a year: around March 20–21 (spring/vernal) and September 22–24 (autumnal).

The word comes from Latin aequinoctium, meaning "equal night." ie day and night are approximately equal in length everywhere on Earth; it marks a point when the Sun crosses the celestial equator, moving from one hemisphere to the other.

Energy-wise, it is a moment of balance and transition.

Solstice also happens twice a year: around June 20–22 (summer) and December 21–22 (winter).

The word comes from Latin solstitium, meaning "sun stands still." In terms of daylight - one day of the year is the longest (summer) or shortest (winter).

Energy-wise, it is a peak or nadir - either expansion and vitality (summer) or rest and inward focus (winter).

Therefore:

Equinox = balance (equal day and night)

Solstice = extreme (longest or shortest day)

The Solar and Lunar Cycles

The two different natural cycles overlap but do not "sync up" perfectly.

Solstices and Equinoxes (Solar Cycle) are governed by the Earth's orbit around the Sun. These are fixed points in Earth's orbit, occurring on the same calendar dates (with tiny shifts over the years).

The Full Moons (Lunar Cycle) are governed by the Moon's orbit around the Earth, where a full cycle is about 29.5 days, this gives 12 or 13 full moons a year, and unlike the fixed solstice dates, the full moon dates drift.

Why They Do Not Line Up
A solar year = ~365.24 days.
A lunar year (12 full moon cycles) = ~354 days.
That ~11-day difference each year means the moon "slides" relative to the equinoxes and solstices.

Only occasionally do they fall close together, and when they do, it is considered especially powerful energetically (sometimes called a 'lunar-solar alignment' or "super seasonal moon").

In spiritual or seasonal practices, this is actually a gift - the solstice/equinox and full moons become two distinct energetic markers:
- The solstice/equinox anchors us in the solar cycle of the seasons.
- The full moon offers an emotional/energetic pulse point, a chance to reflect and align more personally.

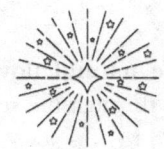

A reminder of the 6 steps to Manifesting with Cosmic Flow

The 'Cosmic Flow Method' combines intentional manifestation with neuroscience, fostering trust, surrender, and intuitive alignment, all in harmony with the natural energy cycles - the natural flow of Cosmic Energy. It helps you manifest by aligning your energy with that of the Cosmos through setting clear, meaningful intentions, evoking emotions, training your brain to overcome limiting beliefs, self-sabotage, and bad habits, and allowing the flow to guide you toward opportunities and synchronicities. All of this aligns with the natural energy given to us via the natural cycles of the Cosmos, the sun, the moon, and the seasonal cycles. It is a natural Flow of life.

Understanding the principal steps of manifestation and the methods to shift your energy, reprogram your subconscious, and align with new possibilities is fundamental.

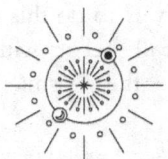

"Change your thoughts, and you change your world"
Dr. Wayne W. Dyer

Align yourself with the natural flow of the seasonal energies by following the workbooks through the seasons.

- Spring - Sow the Seeds of Success
- Summer - Cultivate Dreams
- **Autumn - Align with Gratitude**
- Winter - Release, Rest and Realign

 Review and Reflect
Where are you now, and where are you going? You should ask this at every change of season to ensure you remain on the right path with the new knowledge you have gained. You do this via the Ikiagi and Life Balance Wheel. (Deep live long reflection and trauma release is done with the help of the Winter energy)

 Set Your Intentions
These should be clear and concise. Small intentions can be set at any time, but for big life-changing intentions, use the Cosmic energy of Spring.

 Emotional Alignment
<u>This is the most crucial step</u>. You have to truly feel your emotions to train your brain and heart to see the opportunities the Cosmos will put in your path. The easiest way to do this is via your unique learning style. Energy power boosts will occur with each full moon. (For deep emotional alignment, use the Cosmic Energy boosts of Spring and Summer)

 Trust and Flow
Surrender, allowing the Cosmos to unfold events perfectly and show you the opportunities and synchronicity around you.

 Inspired Action
Act on these opportunities, synchronicities, coincidences and intuitive nudges but without force. These could appear at any time.

Practical Exercise
My Personal Learning Style - Self Check Quiz

Remember, the brain cannot distinguish between an authentic experience and a vividly imagined one. When you infuse your intention with intense emotional energy, your brain (your RAS) begins to believe those experiences are already unfolding and draws your attention to the opportunities.

- Feeling genuine gratitude, joy, or excitement before something happens sends a powerful signal to your brain - it reacts as though the desire has already been fulfilled.

- Emotions act as amplifiers, reinforcing the neural pathways linked to your goals and aligning your mindset, behaviours, and energy with your desired reality.

- This emotional state then draws in people, opportunities, and experiences that reflect it. And your awareness of them grows.

The key is to embody the emotions of your future now - gratitude, love, joy, and excitement. These feelings signal to the Cosmos that your vision is real, drawing that future closer by aligning your energetic state with the reality you want to create.

So how do you do this?

The first thing you need to acknowledge is that we all learn differently, which should be reflected in the tools you choose to evoke emotions. For example, if you are an auditory learner, writing affirmations at great length each day will not evoke the emotions of pleasure, excitement and joy, but will evoke feelings of frustration and boredom, and an auditory learner will have much more success by listening to recorded affirmations to evoke the pleasure, excitement and joy emotions.

Here are the different learning styles. Which are you?

Visual learners - 65% of the population
They prefer to see information to understand and remember it. They often use charts, diagrams, mind maps, and colour-coded notes to help organise their thoughts. Watching videos, viewing demonstrations, and using visual aids can significantly enhance their learning experience. To evoke emotions, these learners will succeed more with 'sight-based' tools.

- Vision boards with emotionally charged images
- Visualisation practices (imagine scenes in vivid detail)
- Mind maps
- Watching inspiring videos or films that spark emotion
- Colour-coded affirmations or journaling
- Creative visual scripting (drawing out your future life)
- Watching your future self like a movie in your mind

Auditory learners - 30% of the population
They absorb information best through sound. They learn most effectively when they listen to instructions, engage in discussions, or hear concepts explained out loud. To evoke emotions, these learners will have more success with 'sound-based' tools.

- Spoken or sung affirmations (with emotion)
- Voice notes or audio journaling
- Guided meditations with vivid language
- Binaural beats and solfeggio frequencies (e.g., 528 Hz, 432 Hz)
- Manifestation playlists or emotional music
- Talking through visualisations with a coach or friend
- Chanting or mantras

Kinaesthetic learners - 5% of the population
They learn best through physical activity and hands-on experience. They prefer actively participating in the learning process, whether building something, experimenting, or using movement to reinforce concepts. These learners often benefit from roleplaying, interactive tasks, or even walking around while studying. The more they can involve their body, the better they learn. To evoke emotions, these learners will succeed more with 'touch and movement-based' tools.

- Embodiment exercises ("act as if" - walk, talk, move like your future self)
- Dance or movement to music that evokes emotion
- Physically writing affirmations or scripting (pen to paper)
- Vision walks (visualising while walking or exercising)
- Creating rituals with physical objects (candles, crystals, symbolic items)
- Roleplaying or acting out your future scenarios
- Sensory anchoring (using smell, touch, and movement to lock in emotion)

Reading/writing learners - Often grouped under visual
They thrive through written words. They absorb information by reading textbooks, taking detailed notes, journaling, or rewriting ideas in their own words. These learners enjoy working with lists, essays, and written exercises and often prefer quiet, independent study time. To evoke emotions, these learners will succeed more with 'text-based' tools.

- Scripting your future in a journal (in present tense)
- Gratitude journaling with emotional depth
- Reading inspirational books, quotes, or stories
- Writing affirmations and repeating them
- Letter to your future self (or from your future self)
- Creating a manifestation journal or planner
- Reviewing written goals daily and reflecting on how they feel

Multimodal learner - 60–70% (overlap with others)
They combine two or more learning styles and switch between them depending on the task or subject. For example, someone might prefer reading to learn new material but find it easier to remember through discussion or drawing diagrams. Being multimodal allows for flexibility, and these learners often benefit from mixing techniques to keep their learning dynamic and engaging. To evoke emotions, these learners will have more success with a blend of styles - feel free to mix and match.

- Listen to your voice-recorded affirmations while journaling
- Create a vision board and describe it aloud
- Meditate while visualising and repeating mantras
- Script by hand, then read it aloud with a feeling
- Dance to a manifestation playlist while visualising your desires

Still not sure which you are - take the quiz overleaf

Just answer each question and keep track of how many times you choose A, B, C, or D. Your dominant learning style will be revealed at the end!

1. When trying to remember something, you usually...
A) Picture it in your mind
B) Say it out loud or repeat it in your head
C) Write it down or read over your notes
D) Try to act it out or physically do something with it

2. In a class or seminar, you prefer...
A) Diagrams, charts, or slides
B) Lectures, discussions, and podcasts
C) Reading handouts or written guides
D) Hands-on activities or group projects

3. When learning a new skill, what helps most?
A) Watching a video or looking at pictures
B) Hearing someone explain it step-by-step
C) Reading instructions or writing notes
D) Trying it yourself and learning by doing

4. Which of these tools excites you most for manifesting?
A) Vision boards and Pinterest mood boards
B) Guided meditations, affirmations, or music
C) Journalling, scripting, or making a plan
D) Dancing, moving, or physically stepping into your "future self"

5. How do you best express how you feel?
A) Drawing, doodling, or using visuals
B) Talking it out or using voice notes
C) Writing in a journal or texting someone
D) Through body language, gestures, or movement

Tally your answers!

A's   B'   C's   D's

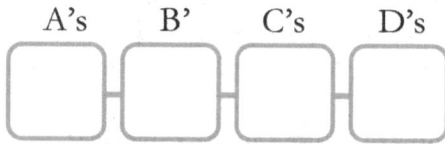

Mostly A = Visual Learner
You learn best by seeing - use visualisation, images, vision boards, and colours to evoke emotion and manifest powerfully.

Mostly B = Auditory Learner
You are tuned into sound - try spoken affirmations, voice notes, meditations, and music to align emotionally.

Mostly C = Reading/Writing Learner
Words are your strength - scripting, journalling, and reading meaningful content will help you manifest with clarity and emotion.

Mostly D = Kinaesthetic Learner
You thrive through doing - use movement, embodiment, rituals, and hands-on techniques to connect emotionally to your vision.

Suggested Daily Routine

Unlike Summer, which is a season of momentum, confidence, and expansion, making it the perfect time to step into the full embodiment of your manifestations or change deep rooted habits. Autumn is a time to reflect on the progress you have made since the Spring, celebrate achievements, and engage in soft reflection. As I mentioned in the introduction, the energy through this season flows slowly through three distinct stages, each offering unique guidance for awareness, release, and preparation.

The keyword for Autumn is 'Gratitude', an often overlooked practice, as negative talk is a much easier practice for the brain! Still, gratitude counterbalances the ease with which negative thoughts can overshadow our successes. From a scientific perspective, practising gratitude ie intentionally noticing and appreciating what we have, activates neural circuits associated with reward, motivation, and emotional regulation.

Gratitude increases levels of dopamine and serotonin, the brain's "feel-good" chemicals, helping counterbalance the ease with which negative thoughts can overshadow our successes. By consciously acknowledging what we have cultivated, we strengthen positive thought patterns, reduce stress, and create an emotional foundation for intentional growth.

Morning Routine
Morning Journaling and Reassessment (10 min)
Use this time to check in with yourself and write freely.
If you are a auditory learner, make voice notes and listen back.
If you are a visual learner make use of your drawings and collage.

Grounding and Gratitude (5-10 min)
Step outside or sit by a window and breathe in the crisp autumn air.
Place your hand on your heart and reflect on
what you are grateful for this season.

Say aloud: **"I honour the process of change.
I embrace reflection, release, and realignment."**

Seasonal Visualisation and Affirmations (5 min)
Picture yourself releasing what no longer serves you,
like trees letting go of their leaves.
Imagine your energy clearing and making space for what is to come.

Repeat affirmations: **"I trust the process.
I release with grace. I realign with my highest self."**

Taking Aligned Action (5 min)
Autumn is also a season of refinement - take one small,
intentional step toward your manifestations.
Follow synchronicities and remain open to new directions and opportunities

Evening
Evening Reflection (5-10 min)
Light a candle and reflect on the progress you have made.

Write down, draw or make a voice note:
One thing I am proud of today
One lesson I learned
One thing I am grateful for

Check in on your weekly task in the
Autumn Workbook (optional)

Nighttime
Practice body relaxation meditation to release tension and align with the slowing rhythm of nature.

Close your day with the affirmation:
(Remember to use your unique learning style - write it, draw it, sing it - most of all FEEL it - knowing the Cosmos is working in divine timing.)

**"I trust the cycles of life.
I release with love and welcome what is meant for me."**

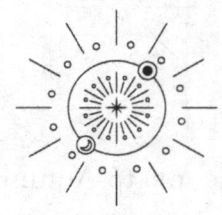

"As the sun sets and the day fades, I honor what has been, release what no longer serves, and open my heart to the quiet wisdom of the night."

Teanna x

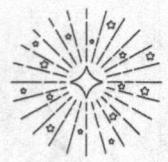

Welcome to Autumn!
Autumn Equinox
September 22nd

The Autumn Equinox marks the official arrival of Autumn in the Northern Hemisphere. Occurring between September 22nd and 24th, this solar event is a moment of perfect balance, when day and night are nearly equal in length. Light and darkness meet, signalling a turning point in the year as the Sun begins its descent toward winter.

Derived from the Latin aequinoctium, meaning "equal night," the equinox represents balance, reflection, and transition. It is a celestial threshold, a pause in the Sun's journey that invites both introspection and celebration. This seasonal shift brings the harvest to completion, energy inward, and attention to what has grown, ripened, and flourished over the past months. Nature slows, colours shift, and the world invites stillness and gratitude.

For those attuned to energetic cycles, the Autumn Equinox is a potent moment to honor accomplishments, acknowledge lessons learned, and release what no longer serves. It is a time to realign with personal intentions, celebrate abundance, and prepare for the quiet, restorative energy of Winter.

Let this equinox be a sacred portal - a space to reflect, express gratitude, and step mindfully into the next phase of your journey.

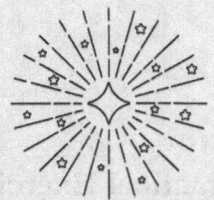

Autumn Equinox Ritual
Reflect and Review

Practical Exercises
Overview of Now
Ikigai - have you found your Soul Purpose yet?
Balance Wheel - what has changed since Spring
Grateful Jar - dive in and enjoy the blessings
Celebrate your achievements

What you will need

Visual Learners
Images, colours, or symbols from magazines, photos, or drawings that represent your accomplishments since spring.
Cardboard to mount on
Glue and scissors

Auditory Learners
A way to record a voice note

Kinesthetic Learners
Nothing

Reflective / Reading–Writing Learners
Paper / Journal
Pen

For the burial ritual
Paper, Pen and open soil to bury your note in
(I like to do this under a fruit tree in my garden, so I can visual all the gratitude as the fruits of the tree grow each year)

Meditation
Embracing the 'Balance of Light and Dark'

Practical Exercise
Overview of NOW

1 Have you discovered your Ikigai - your soul's true purpose?

Yes, it is - _____

If not, review this again on 33. Remember that life is a journey, and your Ikigai can change over time as you gain more knowledge and emotional awareness.

2 Is your Life Balance Wheel truly aligned? If not, you can redo this on 39. Compare it to the last ones you did in the 'Spring and Summer Workbooks' - has it changed in any way? Is it more balanced?

_____
_____
_____
_____
_____
_____

Please note that it is rare to have a continuous 10/10-rated balanced life wheel, as numerous external influences can affect it. However, you can undoubtedly have a more balanced life.

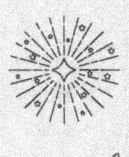

Practical Exercise
Find Your Soul's Purpose

If you found your Ikigai in the Spring or Summer workbook, ***congratulations*** - you have your overall picture. If not (or if you never completed the Workbooks), use this time to reflect again and see what can be added from the last few months. Have you gained new insight? Have you started a new hobby? Did you learn something new?

Remember, it takes time to find your soul's purpose, as you have to learn and gain experiences. This is not a competition - it is a journey we call life.

How it works

The Four Large Circles
(A full-size version is overleaf for you to complete and if this is too small to complete you can print out an A4 version on my website.)

**1. In the circle on the left -
'What you are good at'**
Write down your skills, talents, and unique abilities – the ones you were born with and the ones you learned and mastered during your personal life, work, or education.

Your existing skills, talents, and expertise are essential. Ask yourself what you know well. Everything you have done with good results until now has potential value.

Extra helpful questions to analyse:
- What do I excel at doing?
- Is there something I want to excel at with additional education and experience?
- Which parts of my (current and/or past) job am I good at?
- What am I among the best at within my school/workplace and/or community?

2. In the top circle - "What you love"

Write things you are passionate about, activities that bring you joy, and tasks and topics that motivate you to get out of bed in the morning feeling excited.

You need to ask yourself what fascinates you, what satisfies you, and what you have the most fun doing.

Additional helpful questions to ask yourself:

- What is thrilling to me?
- What could I talk about for hours on end?
- What would I do if I did not have to be concerned about making money and getting paid?
- How would I spend my time on a long holiday or a free weekend?

3. In the circle on the right - "What the world needs."

Note down what your potential clients/community would benefit from but is not accessible to them – or how you can do it better.

What you are offering must be something needed in the world, so you do not end up investing a lot of your precious time and energy into something nobody wants or needs. Analyse what the market/ community needs that you can provide better than your competition (or at least that offers better value to begin with). Is there anything particular that your potential clients/community are trying to accomplish in their work or lives, and what tasks and problems do they want to solve?

Other questions to ask yourself:

- What issues in my community would I like to help solve?
- What matters in my community that I care about, and what problems affect me emotionally?
- Will some of my work be relevant a decade from now, and whose life will it influence?

4. In the bottom circle - "What I can be paid for"

Write down services, tasks, and niches that may give you the most significant return on your time investment and for which you can get paid more.

We have to pay our bills, so no matter what, your Ikigai should not keep you up at night wondering how to stay afloat. It would be a shame to, at best, break even from a 'pricey hobby' that takes up your time, money, and emotional resources.

Some other important questions to ask yourself:

- For what work have I already been paid?
- Are other people being paid for this work?
- Am I already making a good living doing what I am doing?
- If not, according to the current market, can I eventually make a good living doing this work?
- Are people willing to pay for what I'm doing or selling?

The Four Inner Eclipses

Now, you can move to the inner eclipses and note anything that appears in <u>both</u> the bigger circles.

1. Passion – Combines what you love with what you are good at - so write in here anything which appears in both what you love and what you are good at.

2. Mission – In this eclipse, write down anything which appears in both what you love and what the world needs

3. Vocation – In this eclipse, write down anything which appears in both what the world needs and what you can get paid for.

4. Profession – Finally, in this eclipse, write down anything that appears in what you are good at and what could make you money.

Now, look at all these four eclipses - if anything repeats in <u>ALL FOUR</u> - then you have your Ikigai - Your Life Purpose.

If this diagram is too small, you can download an A4 version from my website under the seasons. www.TeannaTaylor.com

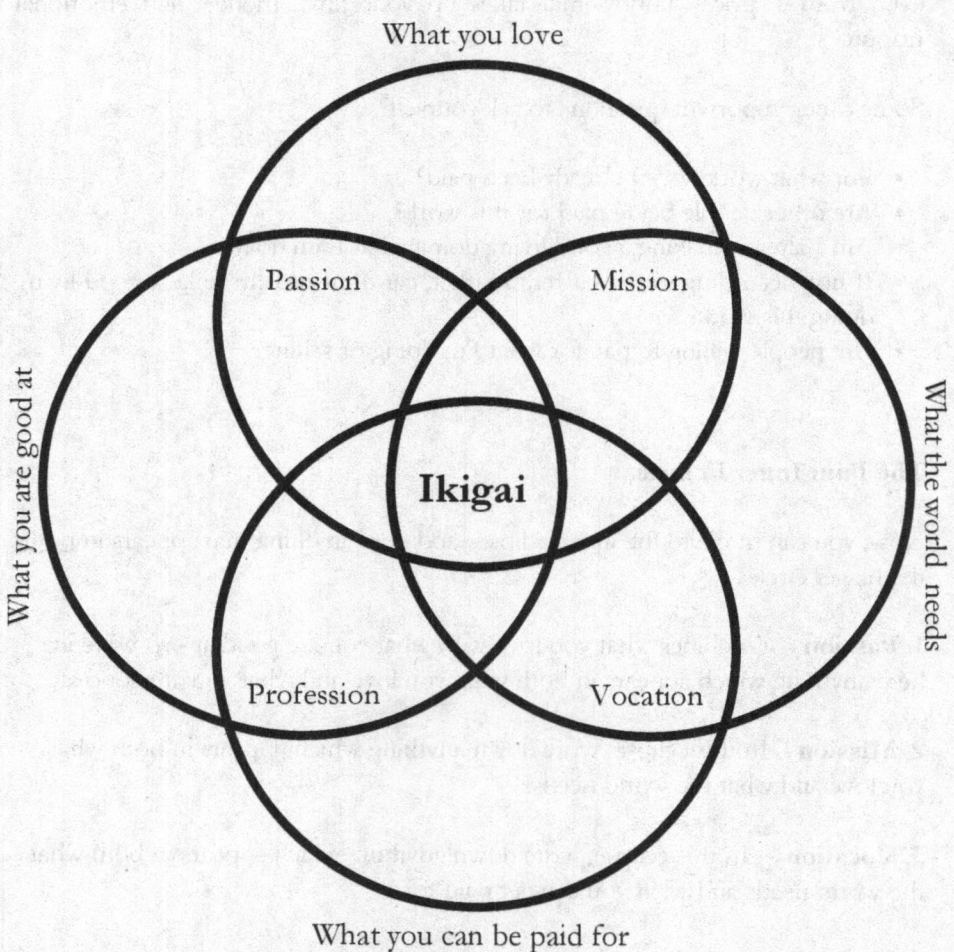

What if you cannot find your Ikigai?

If you did not have anything in all four eclipses - where passion, mission, vocation, and profession overlap - it is entirely okay! It just means you need to explore further.

Here is what you can do:

Reflect on what is Missing
- Look at each of the four sections:
  - What you love
  - What you are good at
  - What the world needs
  - What you can be paid for
- Could you identify which section feels empty or weaker? That is where you need to focus.

Experiment and Explore
- Try new hobbies, volunteer, or take on different roles.
- Learn new skills or deepen existing ones.
- Talk to people in different careers or lifestyles that interest you.

Find Patterns in Your Life
- Think about activities that naturally excite you.
- Please remember past moments when you felt deeply engaged or fulfilled.
- Ask friends or mentors what they think you are great at.

Start with What You Have
- Could you work with that if only two or three sections are filled? For example, if you know what you love and are good at, explore ways to make it worthwhile to the world or monetise it.

Be Open to Change
- Ikigai is not something you find instantly - it evolves.
- Your centre might change as you grow and gain new experiences. - Mine certainly did.

If you did find your Ikigai this time round - ***Congratulations,*** now move on to page 39. If you did not find your Ikigai, reflect on 'what is missing' below. Knowing what is missing can help you focus on those areas to fill them in the coming months. You can then set an intention to address the missing parts.

_____
_____
_____
_____
_____
_____
_____
_____
_____
_____
_____
_____
_____
_____
_____
_____

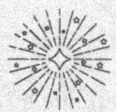

Practical Exercise
Create a Life Balance Wheel

Here is how to do it if you have not done it before
This is a powerful self-assessment tool used to evaluate different areas of your life and identify areas for improvement. It visually represents self-awareness and highlights the balance or imbalance across key life areas. Often highlighting areas where you may feel unfulfilled or off balance. Once identified, these areas can help you set meaningful intentions and focus. It can also be used to track your progress over time.

 **How It Works**
The 'Life Balance Wheel' is typically a circle divided into segments, each representing a different aspect of life. You rate your satisfaction in each area on a scale from 1 to 10, then plot these scores on the wheel. The result indicates whether your life feels balanced or if there are areas that need attention. These out-of-balance areas are typically where your first manifestation intentions originate.

Common Life Areas in a Life Wheel
Though categories can be customised, a standard version often includes:

- Career and Work – Job satisfaction, growth, and fulfilment.
- Finances – Stability, income, and financial security.
- Health and Wellness – Physical and mental well-being.
- Personal Growth – Learning, self-improvement, and mindset.
- Relationships – Love, friendships, and family connections.
- Spirituality – Inner peace, faith, or connection to a higher purpose.
- Fun and Recreation – Hobbies, leisure, and joy.
- Environment and Home– Living space, work and surroundings.

 **What to do**
- Contemplate each area of life and rate it on a scale of 1 - 10.
  1 being completely dissatisfied and 10 being completely content.
- Then, draw a line around the arc or colour in the section from the centre towards the appropriate arc.

Most people first look to manifest those areas with a low score (closer to the center) to bring life back into balance. This is best done in Spring.

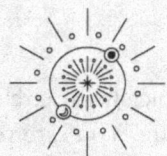

*"When life is in balance,
the heart finds contentment,
and even the simplest
moments feel whole."*

Teanna x

Life Balance Wheel

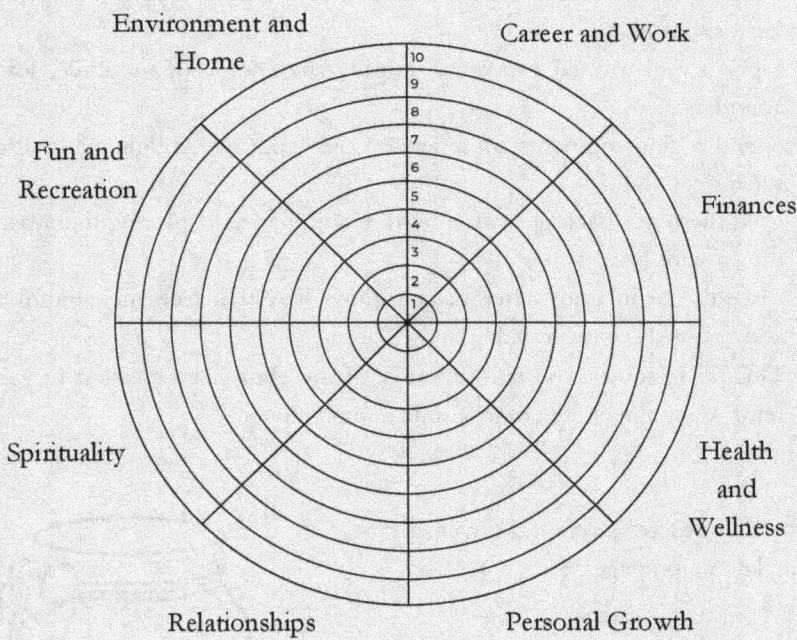

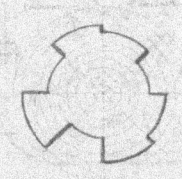

Example

Practical Exercise
Gratitude Jar Review

- Sit down with your Gratitude Jar. (If you have one)
- Take out all the notes and read them aloud, reflecting on the blessings you have received.
- Light a pink or red candle to amplify the energy of gratitude, love, and abundance.
- Spend a few moments in reflection, allowing the feeling of gratitude to wash over you.
- Fold the notes back up with intention and gratitude, placing them back into the jar with love.
- Place the jar in your sacred place or anywhere that feels meaningful to you, and you will see it every day.
- This jar becomes a visual reminder of the abundance present in your life, reinforcing the energy of gratitude and positivity.

If you do not have a jar yet, I cover how to make one on page 58.

Celebrate Achievements
Honour accomplishments, express gratitude and stay grounded amid activity.

What successes or milestones have you reached since Spring? Think back to the end of March, April and May and list every positive thing which has happened or been achieved. Use your Grateful Jar, previous Balance Wheel and Intention list to help.

Visual Learners
Create a Harvest Collage: Gather images, colours, or symbols from magazines, photos, or drawings that represent your accomplishments since Spring, and arrange them on a page or vision board. As you place each one, pause to acknowledge the growth it represents. Keep this where you will see it every day to show you the achievements you have made.

Auditory Learners
Record a Gratitude Voice Note: Speak out your achievements as if telling a trusted friend. Name three things you are proud of, and describe how they make you feel. Play it back later in the week to re-anchor the sense of gratitude and achievement. Save it as an online 'Gratitude Note' and listen back whenever you feel down.

Kinesthetic Learners
Do a Grounding Gratitude Walk: Go outside and collect three small natural objects (eg a leaf, stone, or acorn). With each item, name one thing you achieved this year. Keep these on your desk or altar as tangible reminders of your harvest.

Reflective / Reading–Writing Learners
Write a Harvest Letter: Compose a letter to yourself (or to the Cosmos) listing your achievements. Thank yourself for your efforts and acknowledge the lessons you have learned. Seal the letter in an envelope to open at Winter Solstice as a reminder of your growth.

This way, no matter your preferred style of learning or self-expression, you can celebrate your harvest in a way that resonates deeply with you.

CELEBRATE!

Plan ways to celebrate your achievements, whether through personal reflection, sharing with loved ones, or treating yourself.

I plan to celebrate by:

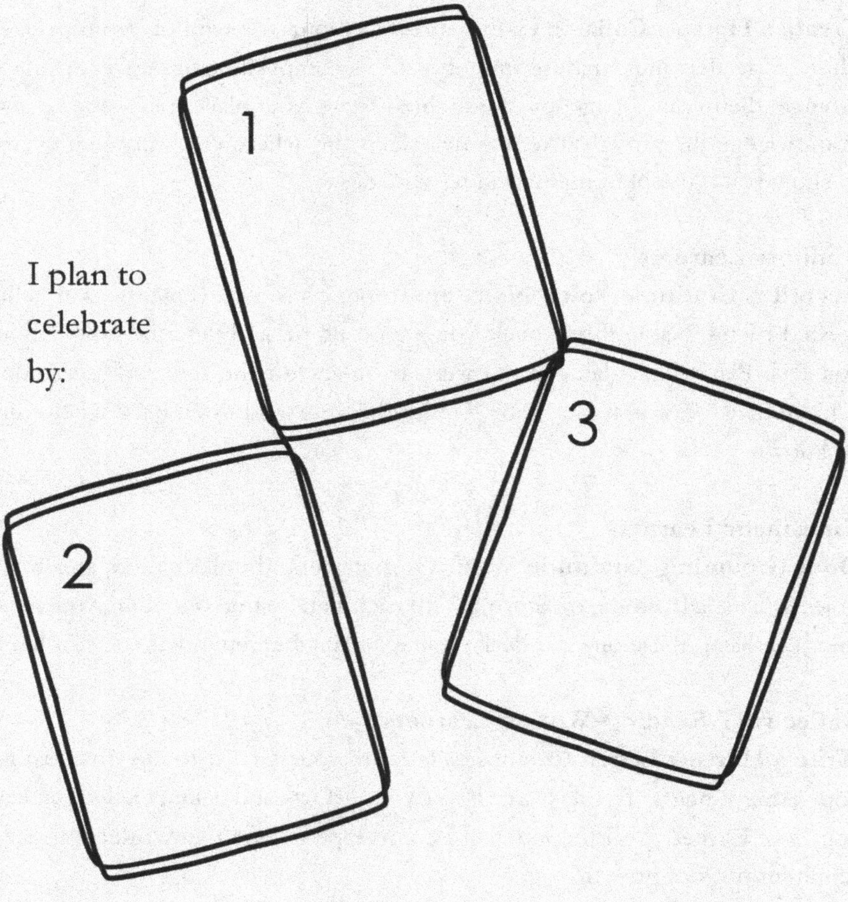

1

2

3

First Quarter Moon
Reflecting on Your Growth
(From 29ᵗʰ September)

Practical Exercise
Write a letter to your future self

Reflecting on all the accomplishments and progress you have made so far. Include advice for the future and your hopes for the rest of the energetic year. (Ending late March before the Spring Equinox)

_____

_____

_____

_____

_____

_____

_____

_____

_____

_____

_____

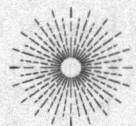

'Hunter's Moon'
Focus and Determination
Reaping Rewards
7th October 2025

The Hunter's Moon traditionally marked a time when communities hunted and gathered food to prepare for the coming winter. Because of its timing in the year and the long, bright evenings it provides, the Hunter's Moon has come to symbolise preparation, focus, and gathering strength.

Energetically, this moon invites us to take stock of what we have, decide what to keep, and sharpen our focus for the colder, quieter months ahead. It is a time for recognising abundance, practising gratitude, and directing our energy with intention. This moon encourages us to acknowledge and protect the things that matter most, honouring their presence in our lives.

Practical Exercises
Reflection Inventory
Preservation Reflections and Letter
Preserve Burial Ritual

What you will need
Paper
Pen/Pencil
Space outside for a small hole
Tool to dig with
Optional herbs - Thyme (courage, confidence, positive energy)
Oregano (joy, vitality, uplifting spirit) Rose petals (love, joy, emotional healing)
Lavender (peace, calm, positivity) Lemon balm (happiness, lightness of spirit),
Chamomile (relaxation, attracting blessings)
or Basil (prosperity, positivity, protection)
Optional - fruit tree to plant

Altar / Place of Focus

For a Hunter's Moon altar, choose elements that honour abundance, preparation, and the balance between light and dark. At the centre, place a bowl of grains, seeds, or a carved wooden bowl to symbolise nourishment, sustenance, and the gathering of resources. Surround it with seasonal offerings such as apples, squash, corn, nuts, or dried herbs to celebrate the harvest's bounty and the Earth's generosity. Add natural elements like antlers, feathers, bones, or acorns to honour the cycle of life, the hunt, and the deep connection between humans, animals, and the land.

Crystals such as carnelian for vitality, bloodstone for courage, smoky quartz for grounding, and obsidian for protection, while candles in deep red, gold, or earthy brown echo the fire of the hunt, the warmth of autumn, and the strength needed for the coming winter.

You might also include incense or herbs such as mugwort, rosemary, sage, or cedar to sharpen awareness and strengthen intention.

Meditation

Listen to the "Gratitude and Inner Strength"

You may also drum, rattle, or chant softly to invoke the primal rhythm of the hunt.

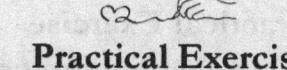

Practical Exercise
Hunters Moon Inventory

Reflect on the things you wish to keep and protect within your life. Especially the new things, habits and relationships, which have come into awareness since the Spring of this year.

Keep and Protect:
Note down things, habits, or relationships that nourish and strengthen you.

_____
_____
_____
_____
_____
_____
_____
_____
_____
_____
_____
_____

Practical Exercise
What Do I Want to Preserve?

Reflect on your growth this cycle and write a letter to yourself; to open in the future. Explain your journey so far, what you have achieved as your awareness has grown, not only what has come into your life but what you have let go of. It is all achievements. Then reflect on what you have been able to give to others - this is your personal gift to the world, a gift which cannot be bought or made - its a gift you give from your soul.

_____

_____

_____

_____

_____

_____

_____

_____

_____

_____

_____

_____

_____

_____
_____
_____
_____
_____
_____
_____
_____
_____
_____
_____
_____
_____
_____
_____

Now choose one or two from the list and letter - and use these for your burial ritual.

_____
_____

Practical Exercise
Full Moon Preserve Burial Ritual

Now you have reflected on what you wish to preserve - set an intention to nurture it - keeping awareness going forward with positive thoughts and gratitude. This ritual helps you embed the positive energy.

Follow these steps to perform a safe and effective burial and preserve ritual.

Prepare your Space
- Choose a safe outdoor location to bury paper safely, preferably under the full moon's light.

Write
- On separate pieces of paper, write down what you want to preserve
- As you write, visualise it embedding into your soul and heart, transferring onto the paper. Nurturing it for the future.

Fold with Intention
- Fold the piece of paper slowly and deliberately.
- As you fold, focus on gratitude. Feel the positive energy.
- Channel your intent into the paper, knowing that it will embed into your heart and soul and strengthen you more in the future.

Bury
- Dig a small hole in the ground with intention - feel the positive energy of the earth as you mindfully dig.
- Place the folded paper in your hole in the ground.
- Add in the optional herbs - as you do smell the herbs and relax, feeling the positive energy of the Cosmos.
- You may also wish to say the affirmation overleaf.

If this is the first time you have ever done this you may wish to plant a fruit tree too - as a visual reminder that positive thinking and gratitude grow your inner gifts. I have a pear tree, which flowers with a beautiful blossom every year and then provides pears - from which a number of babies have been weaned on - including all my four children.

"Under the light of the Full Moon, I preserve what nourishes my spirit. With gratitude, I root my intentions deep into the Earth, knowing they will grow strong and steady. What I cherish is held in love, protected by the Cosmos, and carried forward with me in strength and harmony."

Teanna

Last Quarter Moon
Cultivating Gratitude
(From 13th October)

Practical Exercise
Plan for Giving: Share your abundance with others.

How could you share your abundance with others? Make a list of all the different ways you could share your abundance and then choose one way to act on.

Ways to share with others	I will act on this one
_____	☐
_____	☐
_____	☐
_____	☐

Reflect on the feeling of sharing your abundance with others

New Moon
Cultivating Gratitude
(From 20th October

Practical Exercise
Letters of Gratitude

Write gratitude letters to people or experiences that have supported you. You can use the space in the workbook to decide, record and remember who you are going to write to and why.

_____

_____

_____

_____

_____

_____

_____

_____

_____

_____

_____

_____

_____

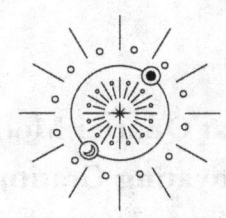

*"When you focus
on gratitude,
everything shifts -
your energy,
your perspective,
and your life."*

Dr. Wayne Dyer

First Quarter Moon
Cultivating Gratitude
(From 27th October)

Practical Exercise
Create a Gratitude Jar (If you already have a jar go to page 60)

You will need
A Mason jar or any decorative jar
Paper or small sticky notes
A pen
-Optional-
Glitter or colourful embellishments
A piece of fabric or string (for decoration)

1. Prepare Your Gratitude Jar
- Find a jar that feels special to you, like a mason jar or any container that resonates with positivity.
- Decorate it using glitter, beads, colorful stickers, or fabric to make it personal and uplifting. I have a key ring on my lock and beads round the outside, as I am not a glitter kind of girl. - Make it personal to you.
- Place the jar somewhere you can see it daily, such as your sacred space, desk, altar, nightstand, or a personal space that you visit often.

2. Set Your Intention for Abundance
- Sit comfortably, close your eyes, and take a few deep breaths.
- As you inhale, visualise the energy of abundance flowing into you. As you exhale, release any feelings of lack or limitation.
- Reflect on what "abundance" means to you - whether it is love, health, joy, opportunities, or wealth.
- Visualise your life blossoming like fruit on a vine, growing more prosperous and fulfilling daily.

3. Write Your First Gratitude Note
- Write down one thing you are grateful for today on a small paper or sticky note.
- It can be big or small - whether it is a moment of kindness, an achievement, or simply the beauty of nature.
- As you write, feel the gratitude within you. Let that feeling of abundance and joy expand in your heart.

5. Practice Daily Gratitude
- Make this a daily habit. Each day, add a note of gratitude to your jar.
- Even on challenging days, find at least one thing to be thankful for.
- By doing this consistently, you train your mind to focus on the positive aspects of your life.

> I also like to add things that come to me or remind me of a
> special day - white feathers, confetti from a birthday or
> wedding, crystals - the 5 pence pieces!
> When I started to write, I was finding 5p's in the oddest
> places - in sealed envelopes, inside photo frames, in my sock,
> everywhere I went, a 5p seemed to appear
> - so all of these are now in my gratitude jar.

If you already have a jar
Take this week to revisit it, and reconnect if you do not use it often - read the notes inside, reminisce with the objects - add in anything you have missed - use the previous week's gratitude inventories and lists to help you - but above all, look at all the positive things you have to be grateful for.

The Science Behind a Gratitude Jar
A gratitude jar is more than just a container of happy memories - it is a tool that works with how our brains and emotions function. Research in positive psychology shows that practicing gratitude can:

- **Rewire the brain for positivity:** Regularly noticing and recording positive experiences strengthens neural pathways linked to optimism and well-being (neuroplasticity).
- **Reduce stress:** Gratitude practices are shown to lower cortisol levels (the stress hormone), helping the body return to a calmer state.
- **Boost mood and resilience:** Studies from UC Davis and Harvard have found that people who keep gratitude lists report higher levels of happiness, improved sleep, and even stronger immune function.
- **Shift attention:** Our brains are naturally wired to focus on threats or problems (a "negativity bias"). A gratitude jar retrains attention toward positive experiences, creating a more balanced perspective.
- **Provide lasting reminders:** Unlike fleeting thoughts, written notes in a jar create a physical record. Revisiting them helps reinforce positive emotions and strengthens long-term memory of good events.

In short, the science shows that a gratitude jar is not just symbolic - it actively supports mental health, emotional balance, and resilience by training the mind to notice and remember the good.

'Beaver Moon'
Forming Foundations
5th November 2025

As we move through into the next moon cycle, you should feel a slowing down of the natural Earth energy, inviting the start of a gentle release and preparation for Winter. This is a time of winding down, where aligning with nature's rhythm helps us move with intention rather than resistance.

Short evening rituals with awareness of the completion of current projects, feeling gratitude for the lessons of the past months.

By attuning to this seasonal flow, we honour both the external cycles of nature and our own inner cycles of growth and renewal. Awareness of these subtle energy shifts, especially in sync with the Full Moons, deepens our experience of reflection, gratitude, and letting go.

In doing so, we prepare ourselves for the restorative stillness of Winter - a time to deep reflection, restore, rest and gently begin again.

The cycle starts with the Beaver Moon, a time when beavers were most active building their lodges and when humans prepared for winter by storing food and warm furs. This Full Moon symbolises preparation, protection, and building strong foundations for the colder months ahead.

Energetically, the Beaver Moon encourages us to reflect on what supports and sustains us, fortify our emotional and physical foundations, and take steps to protect what is important. It is about stability, readiness, and gratitude for the resources we already have.

Practical Exercises
Inner Strengths Quiz
Superpower Reflection
Embedding a Superpower in Daily Life

For your Beaver Moon altar, you could include a bowl of water or river stones to honor the beaver's watery habitat and the flow of emotions. Seasonal offerings such as nuts, seeds, apples, corn, or cranberries celebrate the late harvest and express gratitude for nourishment. Wood, twigs, or bark can symbolise the beaver's lodge, representing protection, home, and the value of steady, careful work. Crystals such as smoky quartz for grounding, citrine for abundance, moonstone for intuition, and obsidian for protection can be placed on the altar to enhance its energy and support reflection, focus, and personal growth during this lunar phase.

Meditation
Listen to the "Roots of Stability" Meditation

Practical Exercise
Inner Strengths Quiz

We all carry unique strengths inside us; qualities that guide how we overcome challenges, connect with others, and create meaning in our lives. Too often, we overlook these inner powers, seeing them as "just part of who we are" instead of recognising them as true superpowers.

This quiz is designed to help you shine a light on those hidden strengths. By answering a few simple questions, you will uncover the core trait that drives you , whether it is creativity, resilience, empathy, or integrity. Each result comes with a deeper look into how that strength shapes your personality, as well as an example of how it shows up in everyday life.

Take your time, answer honestly, and remember: there are no right or wrong answers here. Every strength is valuable, and knowing yours is the first step to using it with confidence and purpose.

1. When you face a tough challenge, your first instinct is to:
a) Look for creative solutions no one has thought of yet.
b) Stay calm and break it down step by step.
c) Reach out and encourage others to face it with you.
d) Remind yourself of your values and stick to them.

2. A friend comes to you feeling discouraged. You usually:
a) Share uplifting words or a new perspective.
b) Help them make a clear plan.
c) Listen deeply and reassure them they're not alone.
d) Remind them of how they've overcome before.

3. When you think of your biggest personal win, it came from:
a) Trusting your creativity or intuition.
b) Hard work, persistence, and problem-solving.
c) Supporting or inspiring someone else.
d) Standing firm in what you believed in.

4. In a group setting, others often notice you for:
a) Your ideas and imagination.
b) Your reliability and steady presence.
c) Your kindness and encouragement.
d) Your integrity and sense of purpose.

5. When things don't go your way, you:
a) Pivot and try something new.
b) Keep working until you find a solution.
c) Lean on your relationships for support.
d) Reflect on what you learned and stay true to yourself.

Tally your answers!

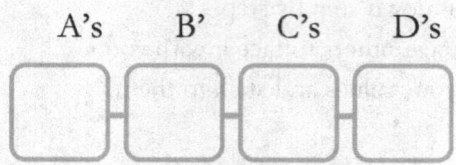

A's   B'   C's   D's

Results

Mostly A's - Creativity and Vision
Your mind sees possibilities that others cannot yet imagine. Creativity is not just a skill for you; it is a lens through which you view the world. You naturally connect ideas, find new angles, and spark innovation. People are drawn to your energy because you inspire them to think differently and expand their horizons. This ability to dream beyond the ordinary is a superpower: it helps you create opportunities, generate solutions in uncertain situations, and light the way when others feel stuck in routine.

Strength in Action: In a team meeting where everyone is stuck, you share a fresh, unexpected idea. Suddenly, the energy in the room shifts. Your creativity opens a path forward that no one else could see.

Mostly B's - Resilience and Perseverance
You have a strength that runs deep: the ability to keep moving forward, no matter the setback. Challenges do not knock you down for long; they fuel your determination. People rely on you because you stay steady under pressure, turning obstacles into stepping stones. This persistence is your superpower: it allows you to finish what others might abandon, to build trust through your reliability, and to model courage in the face of difficulty. Your grit makes you unstoppable.

Strength in Action: On a project full of setbacks, others lose hope. You keep troubleshooting and adjusting until the goal is reached. Later, people realise: it only succeeded because you did not give up.

Mostly C's - Empathy and Connection
Your heart is your compass, and it guides you toward genuine connection. You have an intuitive sense of what others are feeling, and you know how to make people feel valued, safe, and understood. This gift of empathy is more than kindness; it is a superpower that builds bridges where walls might otherwise stand. You have the ability to bring people together, heal wounds, and lift spirits, often without even trying.

Strength in Action: A friend is struggling and feels completely alone. You show up, listen without judgment, and remind them they matter. That moment transforms their experience - your empathy becomes a lifeline.

Mostly D's - Integrity and Purpose

You live with a clarity that others admire. Your values are not just words - they are the foundation of your decisions and actions. This deep sense of integrity makes you dependable, trustworthy, and magnetic. Your superpower is living with purpose: you bring meaning to your work, inspire respect, and lead by example. In times of confusion or uncertainty, you are the anchor that helps others find their footing.

Strength in Action: Offered a shortcut that compromises your values, you choose the harder but honest path. Over time, others see your consistency and trust you even more. Your integrity does not just guide you - it inspires everyone around you.

More than one type?

It is completely normal to see yourself in more than one type. Human strengths are rarely one-dimensional; most of us carry a mix that shifts depending on the situation.

If two (or more) results stand out to you:

- **Celebrate the blend.** Having more than one dominant strength means you can adapt more easily and bring different superpowers into play when life calls for them.
- **Notice the balance.** For example, creativity paired with resilience can help you not only dream up big ideas but also stick with them until they succeed.
- **Trust what feels true.** Read through all the descriptions and ask yourself: Which one feels most like me right now? Sometimes your strongest quality shows up differently in different seasons of life.

Think of it this way: you do not just have one superpower; you might have a whole toolkit. The more you understand each strength, the more you can choose when and how to use them.

Practical Exercise
Superpower Reflection

Now that you know your type(s), ask yourself how does these show up in my daily life? and are you using them to your greatest advantage?

_____
_____
_____
_____
_____
_____
_____
_____
_____
_____
_____
_____
_____
_____

Practical Exercise
Embedding a Superpower in Daily Life

Reflection is powerful, but embedding your insights into daily life is what makes them transformative. The key is simplicity and repetition; rituals do not need to be long or elaborate. Even a 2-minute daily anchor can make your inner strength feel like a living, guiding presence rather than just an abstract label.

Resilient
- **Visual:** Place a smooth stone on your desk. Each morning, look at it and repeat, *"I endure and adapt."*
- **Auditory:** Record yourself saying affirmations like *"I bend, but I don't break"* and play them during your commute.
- **Kinesthetic:** Stand tall, feet rooted, press your hands into your thighs, and take three deep grounding breaths.
- **Reading/Writing:** Keep a resilience journal, end your day by writing, "One challenge I faced today and how I adapted was…"

Creative
- **Visual:** Keep a blank page on your wall and sketch one small doodle a day that symbolises your mood or idea flow.
- **Auditory:** Hum or sing for two minutes each morning to "wake up" your creativity. Optionally, record spontaneous voice notes of ideas.
- **Kinesthetic**: Do a free form dance, shake your arms, or stretch in a new way for 2–3 minutes before starting work.
- **Reading/Writing:** Begin the day with a 3-minute free-write ("morning pages") where you let ideas spill without editing.

Grounded
- **Visual:** Use a calming image (forest, ocean, or candle flame) as your phone lock screen to remind you to pause.
- **Auditory:** Set a timer to play a chime every few hours; when you hear it, stop and take a mindful breath.
- **Kinesthetic:** Practice a grounding ritual: stand barefoot, bend knees slightly, imagine roots growing into the earth.

- **Reading/Writing:** Journal one sentence at night: "The moment I felt most calm and steady today was…"

Connector
- **Visual:** Keep a photo of someone you care about nearby; you see it, send them a kind thought.
- **Auditory:** Each morning, say out loud: *"Today I will connect with someone in a meaningful way."*
- **Kinesthetic:** Give one genuine hug daily or place a hand on your heart while thinking of a loved one.
- **Reading/Writing:** End the day by writing one line about a meaningful interaction you had: *"I felt connected when…"*

Notice how each ritual matches a different way of processing:
- Visuals make your strength tangible.
- Auditory reinforces it through sound and rhythm.
- Kinesthetic anchors it in the body.
- Reading/Writing embeds it in thought and language.

That way, no matter your learning type, you can ritualise your inner strength in a way that sticks.

My 'Learning Type' is

_____

My 'Super Power Type' is

_____

I will embed this by

_____

_____

_____

*"Within you lies a power
older than the stars,
a light that cannot be dimmed.*

*When you turn inward and honour it,
your courage, wisdom, and love are etched
into your heart and soul.*

*This is your true superpower - a force that
grows stronger with every intention,
every act of love, and every moment you
choose to rise in alignment
with your highest self."*

Teanna x

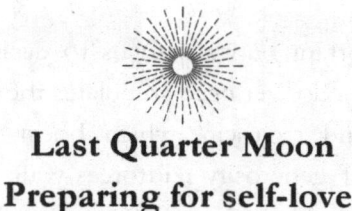

Last Quarter Moon
Preparing for self-love
(From 12th November)

Practical Exercise
De-clutter

Declutter your home - but do it with gratitude. As you release objects, say thank you for how they served you. This act clears both physical and emotional space, showing trust that new opportunities can arrive.

Gratitude focus: **"I am thankful for what has supported me, and I release what no longer serves."**

Physically declutter your home of things that are no longer practical or bring you joy. Donate to charity or sell them.

Then, eliminate unnecessary commitments and distractions as you prepare for winter.

The science
Decluttering is more than just tidying up - it has real benefits for your brain and wellbeing. Research shows that clutter competes for your attention, increasing cognitive load and raising stress levels. A clearer physical environment reduces this strain, helping you feel calmer and more focused. Studies also link tidy, organised spaces with lower cortisol levels, the stress hormone, which directly supports better mental health.

December is the perfect time for this kind of reset. As we move into winter clutter can amplify feelings of heaviness or fatigue. Creating a more open, orderly environment helps counteract the effects of lower light levels and seasonal stress. It also gives a sense of closure and readiness, making space - physically and mentally for the months ahead.

There is also an important outward focus to decluttering. Donating or giving away items you no longer need stimulates the brain's reward system, releasing dopamine and oxytocin, which boost mood and sense of connection. This act of generosity reinforces your values and provides a stronger sense of purpose.

Finally, decluttering is not just about possessions, but also about commitments and distractions. By removing unnecessary tasks or obligations, you protect your cognitive bandwidth and reduce stress on your nervous system. This frees up mental space for what truly matters, allowing you to enter winter with clarity, balance, and resilience.

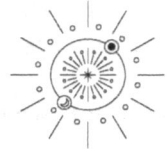

*"Decluttering your home is
not just tidying space -
it is a practice in rewiring your brain.
By removing excess,
you reduce mental noise,
increase focus,
and invite clarity, calm,
and intention into
every part of your life."*

Teanna x

New Moon
Preparing for self-love
(From 19th November)

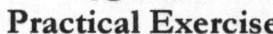

Practical Exercise
Gather and Strengthen Resources

Like the beaver gathering branches, look at what resources you already have – skills, support systems, money, tools, relationships, and express thanks for them.

Then ask:
- What one resource could I strengthen this week?
- Do one small thing to nurture it (practice a skill, reach out to a mentor, set aside savings, etc.)

Visual Learners – Resource Map Journal Page
Draw a central circle with "My Foundation" in the middle. Around it, branch out categories such as skills, people, money, tools, health, experiences. Write or sketch what you already have in each area, then highlight or decorate one branch you want to strengthen this week. The visual layout helps you "see" your abundance and where growth is possible.

Auditory Learners – Gratitude Sharing or Voice Note
Record yourself listing your resources out loud: "I am grateful for my supportive friends, my persistence, my home." Then reflect aloud on which resource you will strengthen this week. You could also share this with a trusted friend or in a group, making the practice a spoken ritual that feels alive through sound and resonance.

Kinesthetic Learners – Resource Collage or Object Ritual
Create a physical collage from magazines, drawings, or objects that represent your resources. As you place each item down, speak gratitude for it. Then, add one image or object that symbolises the resource you will strengthen this week. The tactile, hands-on process lets you feel your foundation as something built and held.

Reading/Writing Learners – Gratitude + Resource Inventory List
Make a simple three-column list in your journal:
- What I already have
- Why I'm grateful for it
- How I will strengthen it this week
- Writing it down helps you process, and you can revisit the list at the end of the week to reflect on progress.

Each one draws on the Beaver Moon's energy of gathering, preparing, and strengthening with gratitude - but channels it through a different learning style.

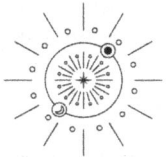

"True abundance begins when you honour the resources already within you - your wisdom, courage, and creativity. By valuing what you carry, you awaken the strength to grow, create, and flourish without seeking from elsewhere."

Teanna x

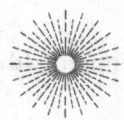

First Quarter Moon
Preparing for Self-Care
(From 26th November)

Practical Exercise
Focus on setting energy fulfillment for you.

Spend time this week reconnecting to your mindfulness practice. Use your learning type to aid the tools and focus. Aim for 5 - 15 mins per day.

Visual Learners
- Guided visualisation: Imagine a peaceful scene or visualise stress leaving the body.
- Mindful drawing or colouring: Focus on shapes, colours, and patterns as a meditative exercise.
- Creating a vision board: Use images that represent goals, emotions, or intentions.

Auditory Learners
- Mindful listening: Pay attention to ambient sounds or music, noticing details without judgment.
- Mantra meditation: Repeat calming words or phrases aloud or silently to focus attention.
- Guided meditation/audio recordings: Use spoken guidance to anchor your awareness.

Kinesthetic (Tactile) Learners
- Yoga or tai chi: Combine movement with breath awareness for a mind-body connection.
- Walking meditation: Focus on each step, the sensation of feet on the ground, and body movement.
- Mindful touch or object exploration: Hold a textured object and explore it fully with attention.

Reading/Writing Learners
- Journaling: Reflect on thoughts, emotions, or gratitude in written form.
- Mindful reading: Slowly read a poem or passage, savouring each word.
- Writing affirmations: Compose short statements of intention or focus to anchor the mind.

Many people are multi-modal learners, meaning they resonate with more than one style. Combining practices, like listening to a guided meditation while walking or journaling, can deepen mindfulness and engagement.

Book a ME day
Simply book a date in your diary for a 'ME' day - aim for a day around the 18th December. This can be alone or with friends - book an entire day where you practice relaxation - spa, concert, massage, meditation - whatever your mind, body, and soul craves for relaxation.

The science
Late November and early December mark a period of heightened stress, especially for women in the Northern Hemisphere, with physiological and psychological indicators peaking in the weeks before Christmas.

Research shows that stress can reduce heart-rate variability, impair sleep quality, and increase fatigue, making it harder to manage both work and personal obligations. Mindfulness practices (even just 5 to 15 minutes per day) have been scientifically shown to reduce stress, lower cortisol levels, improve focus, and enhance emotional regulation.

Tailoring mindfulness exercises to your learning type amplifies their effectiveness. Visual learners respond strongly to imagery and visual cues, auditory learners to sound and verbal repetition, kinesthetic learners to movement and tactile engagement, and reading/writing learners to reflection through words. By aligning mindfulness techniques with your natural learning style, you enhance absorption, retention, and the calming effects of the practice. Multi-modal learners benefit even more by combining techniques, creating a richer and more engaging mindfulness experience.

Booking a dedicated "ME Day" in mid-December is also supported by stress science. Taking a full day to intentionally rest and recharge, whether through meditation, massage, movement, or leisure, can reset the nervous system, improve resilience, and reduce burnout. Research consistently shows that planned recovery periods not only improve immediate well-being but also enhance long-term cognitive performance, emotional balance, and overall health.

In short, this exercise is not just a ritual, it's a strategic, science-backed approach to navigating the peak stress of the season while reconnecting with yourself, your body, and your mind.

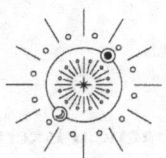

"Mindfulness is the art of being fully present in each moment, noticing the small details, nd honouring the flow of life without judgment. In this awareness, clarity, peace, and gratitude naturally arise."

Teanna x

'Cold Moon'
Balance Stress In Stillness
4th December 2025

The Cold Moon is the final full moon of the Georgian year, rising at the start of the long winter nights. Traditionally, it marked the arrival of the harshest season, when communities would retreat indoors, conserving resources and relying on what they had stored. Its name reflects both the literal cold of December and the symbolic stillness that winter brings.

Energetically, the Cold Moon invites us to slow down, reflect, and turn inward. It is a time for rest, restoration, and clarity - recognising what truly sustains. This moon encourages us to release what no longer serves us, honour the lessons of the past months, and carry forward only what will nourish us through the quieter, darker season ahead. It is about embracing simplicity, practising gratitude, and finding strength in stillness.

Practical Exercises
How do you handle stress - what is your archetype?
Stress Hexagon
Full Moon Release Burn Ritual

For a Cold Moon altar, choose elements that honor the introspective, reflective energy of the season. Place a bowl of water or a small mirror at the center to symbolize clarity, insight, and emotional release. Surround it with seasonal offerings such as dried berries, citrus fruits, cinnamon sticks, or pine needles to celebrate winter's flavors and scents, and add natural elements like stones, driftwood, or pinecones to represent endurance and stability. Crystals such as clear quartz for clarity, amethyst for intuition, garnet for grounding, and selenite for cleansing, while candles in blue, silver, or purple reflect the moonlight and the quiet power of the season. You might also include incense or herbs like sage, cedar, or frankincense to clear energy and invite focus.

What you will need
Small pieces of paper or flashcards
A pen or pencil
A fireproof container (metal bowl / small hole in the ground)
Matches or a lighter

Optional:
Crystals, incense, or other spiritual tools to enhance the ritual atmosphere
Herbs to add to the fire: sage (cleansing), cedar or pine (protection), rosemary (clarity), or cinnamon (warmth and energy).

Cinnamon sticks or pine cones.

Meditation
'Letting go of stress'

Practical Exercise
How do you handle stress - What is your archetype?

The energy is slowly changing as we move closer to Winter, with Georgian December being the peak of stress. Now is a good time to reflect and set boundaries for your personal energy.

Whilst we all have different ways of handling stress, recharging, and caring for ourselves. Sometimes, noticing the patterns in what restores us can reveal more than just habits - it can point to our deeper archetypes, the roles or energies that guide how we move through life.

This quiz is a chance to explore those patterns in a simple way. For each question, choose the answer that feels most like you. Do not overthink it - go with your gut. At the end, see which letter you picked most often and notice what it might say about the type of self-care that naturally fits you best.

1. When I'm stressed, I usually want to...
a) Move my body or get outside
b) Talk it out with someone I trust
c) Retreat into quiet and recharge alone
d) Do something creative or soothing with my hands

2. The self-care practice that feels most natural to me is...
a) Exercise, yoga, or walking in nature
b) Meeting a friend, journaling, or therapy
c) Meditation, sleep, or unplugging from screens
d) Cooking, crafting, or music

3. I feel most balanced when...
a) I've released built-up physical energy
b) I've shared my feelings openly
c) I've had time to rest and reflect
d) I've expressed myself through creativity

4. My biggest challenge with self-care is...
a) Slowing down
b) Asking for support
c) Making time for myself
d) Staying consistent

Tally your answers!

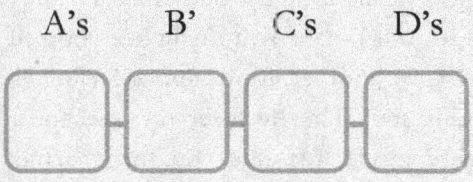

Results

Mostly A's – The Energiser
You thrive on movement and activity. Physical self-care - like exercise, stretching, or outdoor time - helps you release stress and recharge. Action keeps you balanced and reminds you of your strength. The challenge is remembering to slow down, giving yourself permission to rest as well as move.

Mostly B's – The Connector
Relationships are your anchor. Talking, sharing, and feeling supported is central to your well-being. Self-care for you means reaching out, whether to a friend, a trusted listener, or even your own journal. Asking for support does not always come easily, but leaning into connection is what restores you most.

Mostly C's – The Restorer
You recharge best in solitude and quiet. Sleep, meditation, and stillness are your key tools. Self-care for you means boundaries and rest, creating space to retreat and reset. Your natural rhythm is to step back and gather yourself, the challenge is making that time non-negotiable in a busy world.

Mostly D's – The Creator
Your balance comes through expression. Cooking, crafting, music, or any creative outlet helps you process stress and reconnect with yourself. Creativity is not just a hobby for you, it is a form of healing. The challenge is staying consistent with these practices, but when you do, they bring you energy, joy, and renewal.

Multiple Types
Most people will not fit neatly into just one category, and that's the point. These archetypes are patterns, not boxes. You might see yourself strongly in one type, but also recognise parts of another; for example, feeling like The Energiser when life is busy, yet leaning into The Restorer on weekends. Think of your main result as your primary mode, the one you turn to most naturally, and your second-strongest as a supportive mode that helps balance you out. Even the types you scored lower in can be useful to notice - they may highlight self-care practices you have not explored yet but could benefit from.

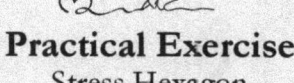

Practical Exercise
Stress Hexagon

The Stress Hexagon makes stress visible and tangible, giving you a starting point for mindful action and better balance in daily life. It is a simple way to visually assess which areas of your daily life are causing the most tension and where balance is needed. Unlike the traditional Life Balance Wheel (where bigger is better), the hexagon works in the opposite way: the smaller the shape, the better. A small, even hexagon means less stress and more balance in your everyday life.

This tool is designed for everyday stress check-ins; things like work, finances, and relationships. These are areas that shift week to week and can often be improved with small, mindful adjustments. It does not measure the "big five" major life stressors (such as bereavement, divorce, serious illness, job loss, or financial crisis). Those events are so powerful they can reshape your life entirely and often require deeper coping strategies, external support, and time to heal.

By using the hexagon, you can quickly see where you are carrying the most tension and where small changes might restore calm and stability.

How to Use Your Stress Hexagon

Step 1. Look at the six areas of daily life:

Step 2. Rate each area on a scale of 1–10:
- 10 = extremely stressful / unbalanced
- 1 = calm, balanced, no stress

Step 3. Plot your scores on the hexagon and connect the dots.
- A small, even hexagon = less stress and greater balance.
- A large or uneven hexagon = areas of tension that may need your attention.

Stress Hexagon

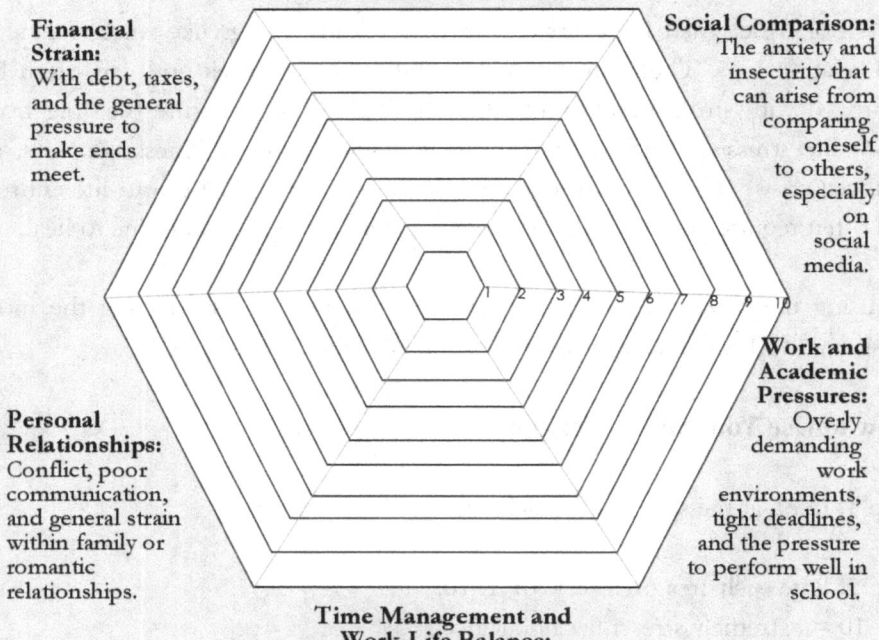

Example

Step 4. Reflect:
Which areas scored the highest (most stress)?
_____
_____

Which areas feel stable?
_____
_____

Work with the archetype to understand why these things stress you out ?
_____
_____
_____
_____
_____
_____

Is there anything you have identified which you could let go of?
Use this for your burn ritual
_____
_____
_____
_____
_____
_____

Practical Exercise
Full Moon Release Burn Ritual

Now you have reflected on why these things stress you out - set an intention to let them go - so the stress goes with them. This ritual helps you let go and make space for new, positive energy. Follow these steps to perform a safe and effective burn and release ritual.

Prepare your Space
- Choose a safe outdoor location to burn paper safely, preferably under the full moon's light.

Write
- On separate pieces of paper, write down what you want to release
- As you write, visualise it leaving your mind and heart, transferring onto the paper.

Fold with Intention
- Fold the piece of paper slowly and deliberately.
- As you fold, focus on letting go. Feel the weight of the stress begin to lift.
- Channel your intent into the paper, knowing that it will no longer have power over you once burned.

Burn and Release
- Place the folded paper in your fireproof container/ hole in the ground.
- Safely light it under the full moon.
- Add in the optional herbs and plants.
- Watch as the flames burn the paper, releasing smoke into the night sky.
- Smell the herbs and relax, as you visualise your stresses floating away with the smoke, dissipating into the Cosmos.
- You may also wish to say the affirmation overleaf.

"I release what no longer serves me. I let go with gratitude, making space for new blessings to flow. As this flame burns, so does the past, clearing the way for my highest good."

Teanna x

Last Quarter Moon
Reclaiming Your Power
(From 11th December)

Practical Exercise
Reflecting on Personal Growth and Self Care

Using the results of your Stress Hexagon from last week's full moon, what is one small action you can take this coming week to ease stress in the highest-scoring area? Once identified, take action and reflect at the end of the week.

The action I plan to take is....

_____

_____

_____

_____

_____

_____

_____

_____

_____

_____

How easy was it to take the action?

_____
_____
_____
_____
_____

How do you feel?

_____
_____
_____
_____
_____

Is there another action you could take to lessen your stressors?

_____
_____
_____
_____
_____

New Moon
Reclaiming Your Power
(From 18th December)

Practical Exercise
Gift to Yourself

Breath, relax and enjoy your ME Day

Embracing Autumn's Gifts as
We Move into Winter

As Autumn draws to a close, it leaves behind the gifts of reflection, release, and deepened wisdom. This season has invited you to celebrate your achievements, honour the lessons of the past cycle, and gently let go of what no longer serves you. Just as the trees have shed their leaves, you too have been called to release with intention, creating space for rest and renewal.

As you transition into Winter, you carry the clarity and gratitude cultivated during Autumn. Winter invites you to slow down, retreat inward, and embrace the stillness that nurtures transformation beneath the surface. It is a time of deep rest, introspection, and quiet preparation for the new cycle that will emerge with Spring.

Winter is also a season of inner healing. Its stillness provides the perfect container for trauma release and shadow work - the courageous act of meeting the hidden or suppressed parts of ourselves with compassion. Here, we are invited to face old wounds, unprocessed emotions, and limiting beliefs, not to dwell on them, but to gently transmute them. By exploring our shadow with honesty and kindness, we reclaim lost energy, release pain stored in the body, and uncover hidden wisdom that strengthens us for the journey ahead.

Honour life's cyclical nature and trust the sacred pause that Winter offers. Autumn has given you wisdom and release; now, Winter encourages you to conserve your energy, listen deeply, and find peace in the quiet. This season teaches us that rest, reflection, and emotional healing are not passive - they are powerful acts of regeneration.

With gratitude for Autumn's gifts, step gently into this season of stillness, allowing Winter to guide you into deeper self-awareness and renewal. Just as nature rests in silence before the return of light, so too do you prepare inwardly, aligned with the rhythms of the earth and the promise of transformation to come.

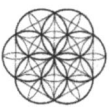

Embrace January
Save Energy -
DO NOT
Set a New Year's Resolution

I cover the reasons for not following the Georgian calendar in much more detail in 'Unlock Your Cosmic Flow' and why making big changes to your life is counterproductive in the middle of Winter when the natural energy around us is one of comfort, deep inner reflection and warmth. Scientifically, in January, the body enters a recovery phase after the intense stress and stimulation of December, where stress hormones like cortisol and adrenaline rise, and although the immediate pressures subside in January, the body often experiences what is called an "allostatic load." This is essentially a stress hangover that leaves people feeling fatigued, unmotivated, and sometimes even run down.

Sleep patterns also tend to be disrupted during December because of late nights, travel, alcohol, and irregular routines. When January arrives, shorter daylight hours in the Northern Hemisphere further disturb circadian rhythms. Reduced sunlight lowers serotonin and throws off melatonin regulation, which explains why many people feel sluggish, flat, or experience symptoms of Seasonal Affective Disorder. (SAD)

The immune system also takes a hit in January. Weeks of overindulgence, stress, and reduced nutrient balance in December can leave the body more vulnerable to illness. Not surprisingly, colds and flu often peak in January, a time when people are indoors more and sunlight exposure and thus vitamin D levels are at their lowest.

Metabolically, January is a reset period. The body is still processing the effects of holiday eating and drinking, such as higher sugar intake and alcohol consumption, which can create temporary insulin resistance and digestive imbalance. This contributes to feelings of heaviness or sluggishness, and it means the body is not at its peak capacity for taking on new demands.

Psychologically, January brings a "holiday crash." After weeks of dopamine highs from socialising, gift giving and festive anticipation, the brain experiences a sharp drop in stimulation. This lack of excitement creates a sense of flatness or even emptiness. As a result, motivation is at one of its lowest points of the year, ironically just when many people pressure themselves to start ambitious resolutions.

For these reasons, January 1st is not the ideal time to set sweeping goals. Energy levels are low, mood is vulnerable, and circadian and seasonal factors stack the odds against success. Studies consistently show that most New Year's resolutions fail by mid-February, not because people lack discipline, but because they choose the wrong moment to begin. The cultural push to overhaul habits at the start of the year creates all-or-nothing thinking, where a single slip-up feels like total failure, leading many to quit entirely.

A better approach is to delay resolutions/intention setting until Spring in March, when the body has had time to stabilise and recover, and the natural energy cycle of renewal begins.

About the author

Teanna Taylor is a compassionate energenics coach and meditation facilitator. Her journey took a transformative turn from a city career when she faced a stroke and endured a ten-year struggle with a debilitating migraine. Yes, one migraine 24/7 for a decade! She discovered the deep connection between mind, body, and energy through the many silent days and meditations. Combining scientific insights with ancient wisdom, she now empowers others through evidence-based techniques from neurology, psychology, quantum physics, and cherished spiritual traditions.

Her story has resonated with many and has been featured in national magazines and newspapers. She has also shared her experiences on an international stage as a guest speaker at global pharmaceutical conferences and has facilitated meditation for over 14,000 people worldwide. Teanna has touched countless lives.

Residing in Whitstable, UK, with her four children, Teanna continues her heartfelt mission to help others heal, awaken, and unlock their highest potential. She understands the difficulties many face and is dedicated to guiding them on their paths to wellness and self-discovery.

Also available by Teanna Taylor

Unlock Your Cosmic Flow
Manifest Your Dreams in Harmony with Nature's Rhymes

Cosmic Flow - Spring Workbook
Cosmic Flow - Summer Workbook
Cosmic Flow - Winter Workbook

www.TeannaTaylor.com

www.ingramcontent.com/pod-product-compliance
Lightning Source LLC
Chambersburg PA
CBHW011127070526
44584CB00028B/3811